This book belongs to

The author and publisher are indebted to Diane Melvin,
Senior Clinical Child Psychologist for the Riverside Health Authority, London,
and NAWCH (The National Association for the Welfare of Children in Hospital)
for their invaluable help in the preparation of this book.

Designed by Alison Fenton

First published in 1989 by Conran Octopus Limited
37 Shelton Street, London WC2H 9HN

This 1990 edition published by Derrydale Books
Distributed by Crown Publishers, Inc.
225 Park Avenue South, New York, New York 10003

Printed in Italy

ISBN 0 517 69197 3

hgfedcba

FIRST EXPERIENCES

Going to the Hospital

Barbara Taylor Cork
Illustrated by Siobhan Dodds

DERRYDALE BOOKS
New York

This is Katie. She is taking care of teddy.
Teddy has a bad earache.
Katie often has an earache, too.
Tomorrow, she is going to the hospital
to have an operation on her ear.

Mom is going to stay with Katie in the hospital.
Katie helps her pack their overnight case.
"Teddy wants to come too," says Katie.
"Here are his pajamas."

The next morning, Katie feels a bit worried.
She is pleased that Mom is coming with her.
Katie doesn't have any breakfast,
because she must not eat or drink anything
until after the operation.

Dad is staying at home
to take care of Sarah, Katie's baby sister.
"We'll come and see you tomorrow,"
he says, waving goodbye.

At the hospital, Mom and Katie walk down
a long corridor to the Rainbow Ward.
"Hospitals smell funny," says Katie.
"That's the smell of all the medicines they use
to make people better," says Mom.

"Hello, Katie," says the nurse.
"Let me show you to your bed."

"Look, there's your name," says Mom, pointing at it.
The bed has sides, so that Katie won't fall out.

"You can put your things in this dresser,"
says the nurse, helping Katie unpack her case.
A little boy, named Peter, comes over to meet Katie.
"Yesterday, Peter had the same operation as you,"
says the nurse. "He's much better now."

The nurse puts a name bracelet on Katie's wrist.
This will tell the doctors and nurses who she is.
"Can teddy have one too?" asks Katie.
"Of course he can," smiles the nurse.

"Come along Katie," says the nurse. "We need to check your temperature and pulse."

She writes down the results on Katie's chart and then takes her blood pressure.

The doctor comes to tell
Katie and Mom
about the operation.
Then she looks
in Katie's ear.

"Now I need to listen
to your chest with this,"
she says, putting her
stethoscope on Katie's skin.
"Ooh, that tickles,"
laughs Katie.

While the other children in the ward are eating their lunch, Mom takes Katie to have a bath. Teddy comes to watch.

When Katie is washed and dried, Mom dresses her
in a special gown for the operation.
"Stand still while I tie the back," says Mom.

Soon it will be time for Katie's operation.
The nurse gives her some medicine.
"In a little while," says the nurse, "you will feel
sleepy and your mouth might feel a little dry."

Soon an attendant lifts Katie on to a gurney
and wheels her to the operating room.
Mom and the nurse go with her.

"Hello, Katie," says a doctor.
"I'm going to take good care of you
while you have your operation.
You will feel a little prick in your hand
and soon you will be fast asleep.
When you wake up, it will all be over."

In the operating room, the doctors and nurses
wear gowns, hats, and masks to keep very clean.

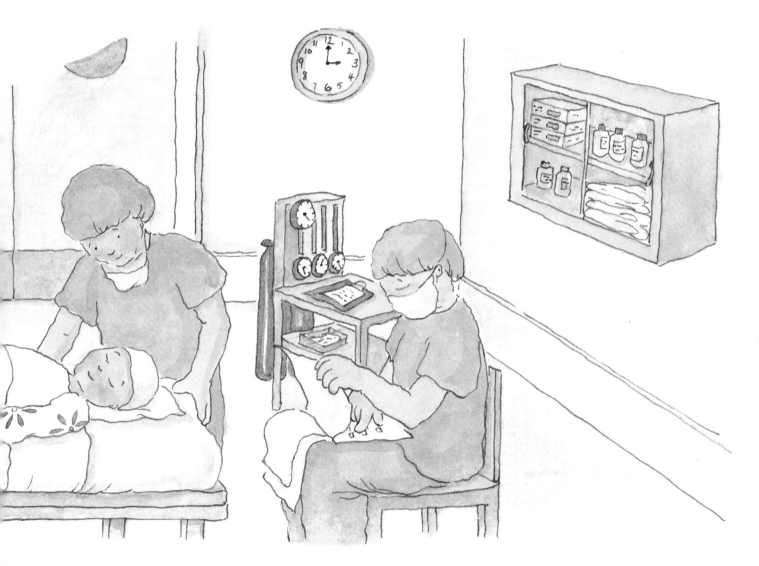

When the operation is over, the attendant wheels
Katie back to the Rainbow Ward.
She is still very sleepy.
Mom sits beside her and holds her hand.
The nurse comes to make sure Katie is all right.

When Katie wakes up, she sees her Mom.
For a little while, she feels a bit sick and
her ear hurts.
The nurse gives her a drink of water
because she is so thirsty.

Katie sleeps well all night.
Mom stays in the hospital, too,
and sleeps in a bed beside her.

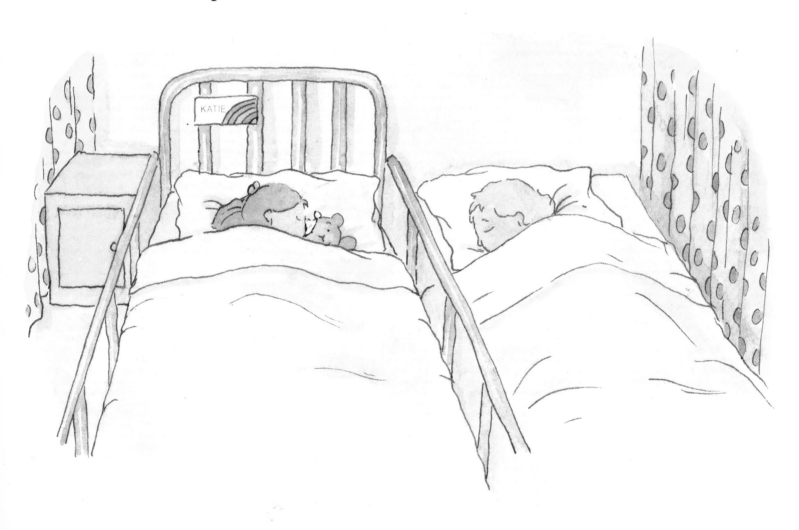

The next day, Katie feels much better.
Dad and baby Sarah come to see her.
They bring her a present and a card.
"After the doctor sees you, you can come
home," says Dad.

Mom packs their case and helps Katie get dressed.
Katie says goodbye to the other children in the ward.
"Thank you for all your help," says Mom to the nurse.

Katie is very happy to be home again.
Her room looks just the same.
"It's nice to have you back," says Dad, and gives
her a great big hug.